PROFILES

NE MISSION · SIX BIOS

WAR SPIES

BY DANIEL POLANSKY

 Sir Francis Walsingham

Benedict Arnold

 Belle Boyd

Virginia Hall

 Allen Dulles

Kim Philby

SCHOLASTIC INC.

PHOTO CREDITS　　　　　　　　　　　　　　　　　　　　　　*Photo Research: Dwayne Howard*

. . . .

Copyright © 2013 by Scholastic Inc.

All rights reserved. Published by Scholastic Inc.,
Publishers since 1920. SCHOLASTIC and associated logos are
trademarks and/or registered trademarks of Scholastic Inc.

No part of this publication may be reproduced, stored in a retrieval system,
or transmitted in any form or by any means, electronic, mechanical,
photocopying, recording, or otherwise, without written permission of the publisher.
For information regarding permission, write to Scholastic Inc.,
Attention: Permissions Department, 557 Broadway, New York, NY 10012.

ISBN 978-0-545-57655-0

10 9 8 7 6 5 4 3 2 1　　　　　13 14 15 16 17

Printed in the U.S.A.　　40
First edition, December 2013
Designed by Kay Petronio

CONTENTS

INTRODUCTION

It is the night before a great battle. The general busies himself with all the many tasks required to prepare for the conflict to come. He looks over maps of the battlefield, memorizing the specifics: hills and valleys and clumps of trees. He double-checks the position of his soldiers and makes sure that each unit is where it should be. He writes letters to his officers, explaining their commands in detail. He makes certain that his army has a clear line of retreat, in case the worst happens and the soldiers are forced to escape. There are many details he needs to make sure of if he hopes to end the next day as a winner.

But of course, the general knows that all of his hard work and planning might end up being pointless. Because on the other end of the battlefield, his opponent is doing the same thing: making his plans, checking on his officers, looking over maps. And there is no way to know exactly what the enemy is planning.

Unless, of course, our general has a spy in the enemy camp! The use of spies goes back to the very beginning of recorded warfare.

In his epic poem the *Iliad*, Homer tells us that Odysseus would sneak into the enemy camp at night, snatching up prisoners and forcing secrets from them. In his famous text, *The Art of War*, great Chinese military leader and philosopher Sun Tzu devotes an entire chapter to the correct way to use spies. In every age and in every war, military leaders have understood the value of spies.

Spies serve different functions, but perhaps most importantly, they steal secret information, known as intelligence, from the enemy. They might also work to sabotage the enemy's plans, either directly or by planting false information. To be a spy means never being able to rest and always having to look over your shoulder. It is a dangerous life, and often short. If discovered, a spy can expect a violent interrogation before being executed.

Of course, there are many different types of spies. Some go undercover in the enemy's camp, stealing secrets and causing mischief. Some become traitors to their country of birth, switching sides and bringing secret intelligence with them. Others might never leave home but work tirelessly to control and maintain networks of secret agents. In this book, we will examine six different spies from six different time periods.

Francis Walsingham was Elizabeth I's chief spymaster. He set up a wide network of spies throughout Europe, who fed him secret information from the courts of foreign kings and queens. He used the secrets he gathered to keep Queen Elizabeth safe from traitors and the country safe from its enemies.

Benedict Arnold was the United States' great traitor during the Revolutionary War. He was a skilled and famous military leader who led the young American armies to victory. But his greed and ambition overcame his patriotism, and he tried to betray the United States to the British. If his plot hadn't been discovered, the newborn American nation might have ended even before it had begun!

Belle Boyd was a Confederate spy during the American Civil War. When her town was invaded by Union soldiers, she decided to fight back in any way she could. Crossing back and forth between enemy lines, she stole secret intelligence from the Union and gave it to Southern officers. She was arrested several times, but always managed to find her way free. For her courage and daring, she became famous throughout the country and even the world.

Virginia Hall was born into a wealthy and well-connected American family, but she always dreamed of foreign adventure. Despite losing a leg in a hunting accident, she went on to become one of the great spies of World War II. First fighting for the British and then the United States, she went undercover in Nazi-occupied France, setting up spy rings and successfully sabotaging Nazi war efforts.

Allen Dulles began his career as a spy during World War II as well, living in Switzerland and working against the Nazis. Unlike Hall, Dulles worked behind the scenes, organizing and running networks of spies throughout German territory. After World War II, he went on to become director of the CIA. In the early days of the Cold War, he worked tirelessly to stop the expansion of the Soviet Union.

As a young student growing up in Great Britain, Kim Philby became devoted to the Communist cause. But he kept his allegiance a secret and joined the British spy service during World War II. Over the course of several decades, he rose through the ranks to become one of the leaders of the British spy service—while passing secret information to the Soviet Union! Philby remains probably the most effective double agent in the history of spycraft, having betrayed untold numbers of British and American secret agents, delivering them into the hands of their enemies.

By learning more about the lives of these six men and women, we'll discover the ways in which the craft of spying has changed over the course of the last several hundred years. We'll also learn about the ways in which the secret actions of one person can have an effect on all of world history.

SIR FRANCIS WALSINGHAM

As an advisor to Queen Elizabeth I, **FRANCIS WALSINGHAM** was responsible for keeping the queen and the nation safe. Walsingham is known as the original spymaster, as he was one of the first people in history to implement spy rings to gain information.

BIRTH AND EARLY POLITICAL CAREER

Spies have existed since the earliest stages of human history, but one of the earliest and most effective modern spymasters was Sir Francis Walsingham. Over the course of his long career, he worked to strengthen the power of the English queen, Elizabeth I. He built a fabulously complex web of spies throughout Europe, and used them to help Elizabeth make wise political decisions that would ensure her continued reign and the success of her nation.

Although in later years he became one of the most powerful men in Europe, Francis Walsingham was born around 1532 to a family with little influence. His family was connected to the nobility. It had money and some presence at court, but not much political power. Francis went to King's College, Cambridge, but did not earn a degree. After spending some time traveling around continental Europe, he returned to England. Back home, he began studying for his law degree at Gray's Inn.

Elizabeth I,
Queen of England

The 1500s in England were a time of great civil and religious conflict. Henry VIII, Elizabeth's father, had broken away from the Catholic Church and founded his own branch of the Christian religion. This made England a Protestant nation, a general term for all of the non-Catholic Christian churches. Englishmen were torn between loyalty to their ancient religion and loyalty to their country. Even the members of Henry's own family were split on the question. In 1553 Mary I became queen of England. Mary was a Catholic and wanted to reverse the changes her father, Henry, had made. She began to imprison rich and

King's College, c. 1880

powerful Protestants, and to make laws that discriminated against non-Catholics. Many Protestants chose to leave England and live abroad. Walsingham was one of them. He spent the next several years living and studying in Switzerland and Northern Italy.

Henry VIII, King of England

In 1558 Mary I died, and her half sister, Elizabeth I, became queen. Elizabeth was a Protestant and quickly set about reversing the policies of her half sister. Those wealthy Protestants who had fled the country returned, Walsingham among them. He had already gained a reputation for being intelligent and hardworking. In 1559 he was elected to Parliament as the member from the county of Bossiney, Cornwall. It would be the beginning of a long and successful political career.

Mary I, Queen of England

In 1562 Walsingham married his first wife, Anne Barnes, daughter of the former Lord Mayor of London. Anne died two years later, and in 1566 Walsingham married a second time, to Ursula St. Barbe, a prominent noblewoman.

There were many Catholics in England who were unhappy to see a Protestant become queen. They disliked seeing Protestants gain positions of power and were concerned that Queen Elizabeth would make anti-Catholic laws. These English Catholics put their hopes in Elizabeth's cousin, known as Mary, Queen of Scots (an entirely different person from Mary I). There were also many people outside of England who wanted to see Mary replace Elizabeth. One of these was a Catholic Italian banker named Roberto Ridolfi. He created a plan whereby a foreign Catholic army would land in England and try to overthrow Elizabeth. With Elizabeth gone, Mary, Queen of Scots, would take charge of the country. To aid his scheme, Ridolfi made contact with important English nobles, as well as with Mary and some of her advisers.

Mary, Queen of Scots

Walsingham was one of the people responsible for discovering and stopping the so-called Ridolfi plot. The intelligence network developed by Walsingham and other top English leaders warned them of what Ridolfi and his partners were planning. Ridolfi escaped, but several of his English associates were captured. Walsingham and others wanted to hold Mary responsible for her part in the plot. But Queen Elizabeth was hesitant to charge her cousin with **treason**, since doing so would result in Mary's execution. Instead, Mary's authority was weakened, and she was put under closer watch.

In 1570, Elizabeth made Walsingham her ambassador to France. Much like England, France was engaged in an ongoing struggle between Catholic and Protestant forces during this period. The conflict in France was much more violent than in England, and would soon lead to a bloody and horrifying civil war. Walsingham was in Paris during the infamous St. Bartholomew's Day Massacre. He watched as Catholic mobs inside the city ran wild, murdering their Protestant neighbors. Walsingham took shelter inside his house and hid other well-known Protestants. This event forever influenced Walsingham's political outlook. He was fearful that a similar event would take place in England should the Catholic forces ever regain power. Walsingham would spend the rest of his political career trying to weaken

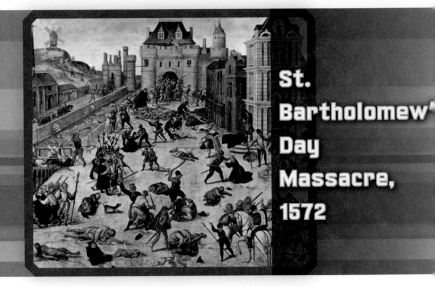

St. Bartholomew' Day Massacre, 1572

the power of the foreign Catholic nations, and ensuring that the Catholic forces within England remained weak and divided.

RISE TO POWER

In 1576 Walsingham became Elizabeth's Principal Secretary in the Privy Council of England. This title meant Walsingham was the chief person responsible for creating and putting into practice Elizabeth's political policies. It essentially made him the second-most-powerful person in England, after the queen herself.

In addition to his normal political duties during this

time, Walsingham began to build his huge network of informers and secret agents that would make him famous throughout Europe. Walsingham was not a spy in the popular sense of the word. After becoming Elizabeth's Principal Secretary, he rarely left England, and certainly did not engage directly in any spying. Rather, he was what is sometimes called a spymaster, meaning that he directed the efforts of a large ring of spies. He was responsible for analyzing the information they provided, pointing them at targets, and making political decisions based on the secret intelligence he had acquired.

This was several centuries before anyone thought of having an official intelligence service. There were no training programs for spies, nor a clear system of control over them. The spies that Walsingham recruited came from a wide segment of society, and they reported to him personally. He had many informers throughout England and across Europe. Walsingham bought the loyalty of the friends of foreign diplomats, their maids and servants, and anyone who could provide him with information that might be useful. Walsingham also had professional agents working for him. Some were experts in cryptography, meaning the science of making and breaking hidden codes. Others were skilled at secretly opening and resealing letters, something that Walsingham used to great effect during his career.

The rest of the European nations had a similar policy toward spycraft. Walsingham needed to always be careful that his own secrets weren't spread by spies working for France, Spain, or the other Catholic countries. Walsingham was a genius master spy because of his ability to determine who among his followers was honest and who might betray him. He was also skilled at corrupting the agents of enemy powers.

Politically, Walsingham saw Protestant England as an opposite to Catholic Spain. Spain was larger in terms of land and population, and had a much stronger army. But England had a more powerful navy and was growing wealthy from international trade. Walsingham worked to support other Protestant nations in Europe, primarily the Netherlands, providing money and intelligence. He hoped that doing so would weaken and distract the Spanish Empire.

Within England, Walsingham took the lead in actively silencing followers of the Catholic faith. Powerful Catholics, including some secret priests, were imprisoned and sometimes even executed. Walsingham was always concerned about the possibility that the powerful Catholic nobility would rebel against the queen. And after seeing what had happened in Paris during the St. Bartholomew's Day Massacre, he feared the violence that would erupt in England during a civil war.

The British armada, 1588

By today's standards, Walsingham's actions against English Catholics were quite horrible. In his defense, however, there were many nobles who sought to **dethrone** Elizabeth. One of these nobles was Sir Francis Throckmorton, cousin of one of Elizabeth's ladies-in-waiting. Similar to the earlier Ridolfi plot, the Throckmorton plot relied on Spanish gold and French soldiers to encourage a revolt within England that would result in Mary, Queen of Scots, on the throne. After hearing rumors of this plot through his intelligence network, Walsingham managed to plant a spy in the French embassy in London. This spy alerted Walsingham to a suspicious meeting between Throckmorton and the French ambassador. After hearing of this meeting, Walsingham ordered that Throckmorton be followed by some of his spies. These spies ultimately discovered evidence in Throckmorton's house uncovering his treason. Walsingham ordered Throckmorton tortured, during which he confessed to the remaining details of the plot. Throckmorton was executed, and the French ambassador was exiled from England.

Once again, Elizabeth was unwilling to order her cousin's death. Instead, Mary was stripped of her right to become queen and imprisoned. Walsingham also insisted on creating what was called the Bond of Association. This was a law that essentially guaranteed that Mary would be put to death if she was again found guilty of plotting against Elizabeth.

Of course, as one of Elizabeth's chief advisers, Walsingham had many responsibilities besides spycraft. He encouraged colonization in North America and elsewhere. Walsingham recognized early on the importance of international trade and exploration, both for its own sake and as a way of weakening the Spanish Empire. Spain had been the first European power to explore the far reaches of the globe, financing Christopher Columbus's expedition to the New World in 1492. It had grown fabulously wealthy from its colonies in South America, stealing vast amounts of gold, silver, and precious minerals from the native peoples there. However, the Spanish Empire had grown so quickly that it could not be easily defended. It had colonies and cities throughout South America and in Southeast Asia. But it did not have enough ships or men to protect them.

In this era, there was little difference between trade and piracy. By encouraging foreign exploration, Walsingham hoped that English forces would attack the very source of Spain's great wealth and power. He supported Sir Francis Drake's 1577 round-the-world voyage, during which Drake captured many Spanish ships and gained great wealth for England. Soon English raiders could be seen throughout the world, stealing the riches of the Spanish Empire.

WAR AGAINST THE SPANISH

By the 1580s the long-simmering tensions within Europe erupted into open violence throughout the continent. The conflict that came to dominate European politics in this period was called the Eighty Years' War. It was between the Spanish Empire and the mostly Protestant Netherlands. The Netherlands had been a part of the Spanish Empire but rebelled against the anti-Protestant policies of Spanish

King Philip II. In 1584 the leader of the Protestant forces in the Netherlands, William of Orange, was assassinated by a Catholic fanatic supported by the Spanish. This criminal act sent shock waves throughout Europe. Assassination at this point in European history was rare. Even the most determined enemies were reluctant to order the murder of another king or queen.

William of Orange

Walsingham had long pushed for England to actively support the Dutch rebels. Queen Elizabeth and some of her other advisers, however, were reluctant to anger the Spanish by doing so. The death of William of Orange pushed Elizabeth and her more conservative advisers to act. They signed the Treaty of Nonsuch in August 1585, which sent English troops to help fight the Spanish in the Netherlands.

There were many secret Catholics living in England at this point, and the possibility that one of them might attempt to assassinate Elizabeth could not be ignored. Walsingham continued to be fearful of the potential for

Mary, Queen of Scots, to unite pro-Catholics and lead the country to civil war. After her two failed attempts to do just that, Mary had been exiled to a large mansion in Chartley. Walsingham did not trust her and kept her under close watch. Her letters were opened and read before being passed to her, a precaution meant to ensure that she could not engage in any plotting. Realizing what was happening, Mary came up with a secret method of correspondence. She would hide her letters in a beer cask and then have the cask sent out of her house.

Walsingham discovered this ploy. But he allowed it to continue as a way of keeping watch on Mary's activities, hoping that she would do something to incriminate herself. He did not have long to wait. A wealthy Catholic nobleman named Anthony Babington contacted Mary using this "secret" method, saying that he and a group of friends were planning to murder Elizabeth. Mary agreed to the plan. What neither realized was that one of the plotters was already a secret agent for Walsingham, who knew about the entire conspiracy. Babington and his followers were rounded up and executed.

Mary's fate was more complicated. She insisted that the entire plot had been created by Walsingham himself, and that she was an innocent victim of his schemes. A special court created to judge the situation found her guilty

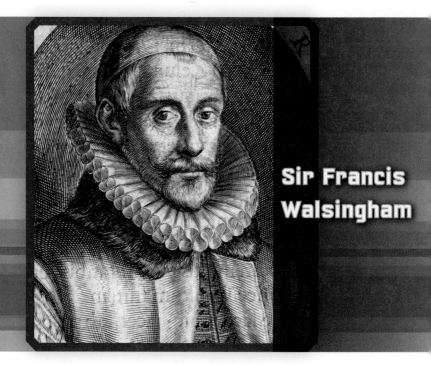

Sir Francis
Walsingham

of plotting to assassinate the queen. Under the Bond of Association, this meant an automatic sentence of death. Queen Elizabeth was still uncomfortable with ordering her cousin's death despite the pressure Walsingham put on her and her legal obligation to do so. Elizabeth seemed to recognize the necessity of executing a cousin who conspired against her many times, but she did not want the blood of a cousin on her hands. She signed the warrant for Mary's execution, then gave it to William Davison, the junior secretary of state, with unclear instructions on what to do with it. Davison decided to give it to the Privy Council, who agreed to carry out the sentence.

Mary, Queen of Scots, was beheaded on February 8, 1587. When Elizabeth found out, she was furious, even going so far as to imprison Davison. Over time her anger cooled, however, and Walsingham managed to get Davison freed.

It was an ugly episode, and there is still some question about the degree to which Mary's involvement in the plot was managed by Walsingham. But Walsingham always put the interests of his country ahead of his own personal sense of right and wrong. As far as Walsingham was concerned, Mary's very existence was a danger to Elizabeth and to the country. As long as she lived, she gave the Catholic resistance a figurehead, and inspired violence against the queen. Her execution was necessary to keep the country safe, and he never regretted it.

Perhaps Walsingham's greatest success was his role in defeating the legendary Spanish armada. By the mid-1580s Philip II was tired of England thwarting his plans to dominate Europe. He had been humiliated by English naval raids on Spanish cities. He was also furious at England's continued support for the brave Dutch rebels. Finally, he was angered by the execution of Mary, Queen of Scots. Philip decided he needed to strike a blow against England. He began to build a vast fleet of ships, called an

Defeat of
the Spanish
armada, 1588

armada, the largest in European history. His goal was to send a Spanish army into England to overthrow Elizabeth and make him king.

Philip's plans were made with the greatest possible secrecy, but all the same Walsingham began to hear rumblings from across the vast network of spies and intelligence agents he had created. He had recruited a friend of the Tuscan ambassador to Madrid as a spy, and the information he received proved very valuable. Because of the early warning Walsingham's spies provided, England was able to prepare for the armada's attack. Walsingham provided money to rebuild Dover Harbor, which gave the English navy a base from which it could respond quickly to a Spanish attack. He encouraged Drake's naval raid on the Spanish city of Cadiz, which slowed Spanish preparations for war. He also ordered the English ambassador to the Ottoman Empire to encourage attacks on Spanish possessions. He did everything possible to weaken and distract the Spanish.

When the Spanish armada sailed for England in July 1588, it found a country that was well prepared for its attack. After a series of small battles off the English coast, the armada anchored off the small port of Gravelines. The English, led by Walsingham's old ally Drake, set loose a number of fireships against the armada. These were special boats that were packed with explosives, then set to drift toward the Spanish fleet and abandoned. The use of the fireships was a tremendous success. The armada was defeated and England was saved. Afterward, naval commander Lord Henry Seymour wrote to Walsingham,

"You have fought more with your pen than many have in our English navy fought with their enemies."

Depiction of an English
warship attacking the
Spanish armada, 1588

It was a fitting compliment for one of the directors of the
English victory.

DECLINE AND DEATH

Walsingham had long suffered from health issues that
made it necessary for him to leave court for long periods
of time. By the time of the defeat of the Spanish armada,
he was near death. On April 6, 1590, he died in his house
on Seething Lane, of what was probably cancer. He had
spent huge sums of money in England's service, and he

died owing the Crown more than £40,000. In recognition of his service, Elizabeth canceled the debt and granted his daughter a yearly pension.

History looks back on Walsingham with somewhat mixed views. Some criticize his actions against English Catholics as being unjust and brutal, although this was a time when religious minorities were persecuted throughout Europe.

Chart of the Spanish armada's course, 1588

Francis
Walsingham

Others point to the critical role he played in defeating
Spain, strengthening the English monarchy, and helping
England grow from a minor European power to an empire
that spanned the globe. But regardless of the questionable
morality of Walsingham's actions, he was without question

the great spymaster of his time. His network of agents within Europe was unrivaled. More importantly, he was successful in long-term thinking, promoting England's overseas trading network and pushing England to assume its role as an opponent to the Spanish Empire.

BENEDICT ARNOLD

BENEDICT ARNOLD is known as the greatest American traitor of all time. Originally a successful general in the Revolutionary War, Arnold switched sides to help the British to sabotage his homeland.

EARLY YEARS

Benedict Arnold, the United States' most infamous traitor, betrayed his country and dishonored his heroic reputation for the sake of greed and personal ambition.

Arnold was born in Norwich, Connecticut, on January 14, 1741, to parents Benedict and Hannah. One of his ancestors had been the governor of Rhode Island and both sides of his family had deep roots in the area. He had five brothers and sisters, though only he and one sister survived to adulthood.

By the time Arnold was in his early teens, his family's fortunes had taken a turn for the worse, as his father had foolishly wasted away the money he had made. Soon there was nothing left to pay for Arnold's education. Arnold's beloved mother used her family connections to get Arnold an apprenticeship with her cousins at a small pharmacy. When the French and Indian War broke out, Arnold briefly served in the local militia but was never in combat.

By 1762 Arnold had completed his apprenticeship and he opened a pharmacy and bookshop in New Haven, Connecticut. Arnold was smart and worked hard, and soon had so much success that he was able to buy back his family's home, which his father had been forced to sell years earlier. In 1764 Arnold started a partnership with another Connecticut merchant, buying three ships for trade with the West Indies. Arnold would often serve as captain on his ships, going on long trading voyages. During one of them, Arnold fought and won a duel with a British captain who had shown disrespect for the American colonies.

MOVING TOWARD REVOLUTION

The American colonies in the mid-eighteenth century were a tumultuous place. The thirteen colonies, which began as individual communities on the east coast of North America, were growing larger and richer. They demanded greater independence from the British homeland. The British thought the colonies were irresponsible and ungrateful. They saw the relationship between Great Britain and the colonies as being like that of a parent and a child. The colonies existed to make Great Britain richer, and colonists did not deserve political representation or the same rights as those granted to people living in Great Britain.

Needing money to finance its growing empire, the British Parliament passed a series of special taxes that it demanded the colonists pay. The first was on sugar in 1764 and the second on stamps in 1765. These taxes were tremendously unpopular in the colonies. They made basic goods more expensive, but more importantly, many colonists felt it was fundamentally unjust that they were required to follow laws they had no role in making. "No taxation without representation" became the colonists' rallying cry.

Like many others, Arnold disliked the new taxes and showed this dislike by actively ignoring them. He used his boats to ship goods without paying for the stamps the law required. When a man informed the authorities of Arnold's crimes, he and several followers attacked the man. Arnold was arrested, but the taxes were so unpopular, and informers so disliked, that he was only given a small fine.

In 1767 Arnold married for the first time, to Margaret Mansfield. She gave birth to three children: Benedict,

Stamp Act 1765 protest, New York City

Richard, and Henry. Sadly, Margaret died in 1775, shortly after the outbreak of the war between the colonies and Great Britain.

THE COLONIES GO TO WAR

By 1774 the long-simmering disagreements between the colonies and Great Britain had reached a boiling point. The British leaders felt provoked by the colonists' continued refusal to pay taxes, as well as by their anti-British writings and protests. King George III and his advisers felt confident that the colonists were all talk. They did not think that the colonists would be able to fight against the might of the British Empire. They passed a royal **decree** stating that the rebellious colonists were criminals, making war a certainty.

The British had good reason for disrespecting the fighting power of the American colonies. The colonies had no standing army, only small militias, each serving its own area. These militias were often poorly trained and equipped. The colonists themselves were still working out a system of government. It was unclear if the individual colonies would be able to put aside their differences and work together for the common good.

Against this disorganized band of colonials, the British had a professional army, backed by the greatest navy in

Colonists confronting
British soldiers

the world. The British Empire spanned the globe, and was the richest and most powerful in the world. Despite this, Britain had much to be worried about in going to war against the Americans. The sheer size of America made military operations tremendously difficult. The British had to ship their supplies and reinforcements all the way across the Atlantic Ocean. Once they landed, they found themselves in the midst of a largely unfriendly territory, several times as large as Britain, with poor roads and a huge countryside to travel through.

At the beginning of the war, however, it seemed certain to most that the mighty British Empire would be too much for the colonists. But this did not frighten Arnold, who quickly enlisted as a captain in the New Haven militia. When news of the Battles of Lexington and Concord reached New Haven, Arnold and the militia wanted to march to Massachusetts to assist their fellow colonists. When the New Haven town council refused permission, Arnold threatened to break into the armory and take weapons and ammunition to Lexington and Concord. The town leaders backed down, and Arnold and his men began their march toward Massachusetts.

While on the march, Arnold came up with the idea of making a surprise attack on Fort Ticonderoga, in upstate New York. He managed to convince the Massachusetts Committee of Safety to support the plan, and they made him colonel in the Massachusetts militia. He led a small group of soldiers toward Fort Ticonderoga, but on the way met another militia leader also planning to attack the fort. After some bickering, the two agreed to join forces.

On May 10, 1775, Arnold and his men surprised the small group of British soldiers at Fort Ticonderoga, capturing it without a battle. They then went on to capture two nearby forts. But in June a larger force of American soldiers arrived to take control of the fort. This meant that Arnold would no longer be in command. Rather than accept that, Arnold resigned and went home.

The attack on Fort Ticonderoga showed what would become the two most defining features of Arnold's character. He was a skilled military leader, courageous and quick to act. He was also vain and easily insulted. He disliked working under others and his ambition often got the better of him.

WAR HERO

After leaving Fort Ticonderoga, Arnold looked for another

Fort Ticonderoga, present day

expedition to lead. He convinced George Washington, then the commander in chief of the Continental Army, to launch an attack on Quebec City, and to let Arnold lead it. Arnold was made a colonel in the Continental Army. With 1,100 men under his command, he began to march through the Maine wilderness. It was a difficult passage. Many of his soldiers died or turned back.

By November, however, Arnold and his men had completed the long march north. They joined forces with another small American army, led by Richard Montgomery. The two launched their combined armies on Quebec City in late December 1775.

The attacks were a disaster. A small number of British and Canadian troops fought off the American army. Montgomery was killed and Arnold was injured. He pulled his troops back, and led an unsuccessful attack against Quebec City until he withdrew in May 1776. For leading a troop of men such a great distance, he

General George Washington

was promoted to brigadier general.

This was a period of time when advancement in the army had more to do with knowing the right politicians than it did with being a skilled military leader. Arnold played this game as actively as anyone, but he was not always successful. He was also aggressive and continued feuding with other officers.

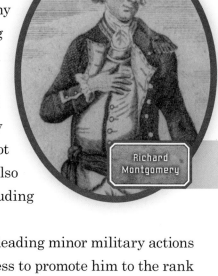

Richard Montgomery

Arnold spent the next year leading minor military actions and trying to convince Congress to promote him to the rank of major general. When this promotion did not come quickly enough, he several times tried to resign. But Washington, recognizing Arnold's talent as a military leader, persuaded him to stay. After Arnold was finally promoted to major general, Washington sent him to New York.

Arnold arrived at a very dangerous time for the colonists. The British had a new plan. They were going to try to separate the New England colonies, considered the most anti-British, from the rest of the country. They sent an army under General John Burgoyne to march from Canada down to the Hudson River.

Fighting against General Burgoyne was a portion of the
Continental Army and a large force of colonial militia, led
by General Horatio Gates. Gates was a terrible soldier:
cowardly, weak-willed, and more concerned with his own
reputation than he was with the lives of his men or the
success of his mission. When Arnold arrived in August, he
and Gates did not get along.

On the British side, however, things did not look much
better. Burgoyne and his soldiers were in a dangerous
situation. Winter was coming, and Burgoyne knew that if
he did not find a place to build camp, his men would die in

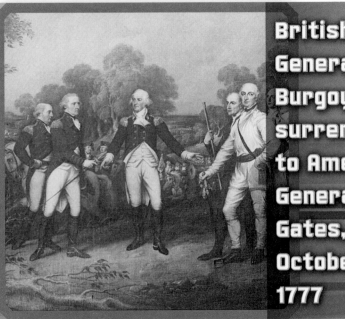

British
General Joh
Burgoyne
surrenders
to American
General
Gates,
October 17,
1777

the frigid wilderness. He decided to march toward Albany, hoping to capture it quickly and then use it as a base to spend the winter.

The colonial army took up a strong position at Saratoga and waited for the British army to arrive. Arnold saw the opportunity to send a small force of men at the weak British flank. Gates, typically a very cautious leader, unhappily agreed. Arnold's tactic was effective, but the remainder of the battle was fought to a bloody tie.

Over the course of the next few days, Gates and Arnold's relationship went from bad to worse. Gates refused to give Arnold any credit in the official report of the first battle. This resulted in a huge fight between the two, and Gates removed Arnold from command.

On October 7, a few weeks after the first battle, the British struck again. The battle was still very much in doubt when Arnold, despite being no longer in command, led a force of men against the British troops. Though Gates sent a messenger to pull Arnold back, Arnold continued to press forward. His attack was a great success, breaking through the British troops and capturing many soldiers. While in the middle of it, however, Arnold's horse was hit with cannon fire, and collapsed on top of Arnold. This shattered Arnold's leg, and though it was not amputated, he was never able to walk easily again.

The Battle of Saratoga was one of the turning points of the Revolutionary War. The large number of soldiers lost deeply humiliated the British. More importantly, the success convinced the French that the colonists had a real chance of defeating the British. The French began negotiating to enter the war on the side of the colonies.

BITTERNESS AND BETRAYAL

Arnold never felt that he received enough credit for his heroism at Saratoga. Gates conspired to make himself look like the hero of the battle, though the other officers agreed that it was Arnold who had saved the day. Regardless, with his injured leg Arnold could not continue as a battlefield commander. He was made military commander of Philadelphia, which the British had occupied from September 1777 through June 1778.

Arnold soon began to engage in a series of business dealings that some considered unethical, if not illegal. He attempted to make money using the political position he had been granted. In fairness to Arnold, this was somewhat

Benedict Arnold

common practice at the time. All the same, it resulted in a court-martial. The court-martial found Arnold to be not guilty of most of the serious charges against him, but it still hurt his reputation. He wrote to Washington that "having become a cripple in the service of my country, I little expected to meet [such] ungrateful returns."

While in Philadelphia, Arnold married Margaret "Peggy" Shippen, the eighteen-year-old daughter of a judge and major business leader who was also a prominent British Loyalist. While the British had occupied Philadelphia, Shippen had made the acquaintance of many important British officers and leaders. Arnold now began a series of actions that would turn him from a war hero to perhaps one of the most hated Americans who ever lived. Arnold was bitter at being passed over for promotions and angry that his honor had been damaged by the criticisms of his financial dealings. He also thought that it was unlikely that America would ultimately win the war against Britain, and he wanted to be on the winning side. Finally, he had run up substantial debts in Philadelphia and hoped to find some way to pay them.

Using his wife's contacts, Arnold got in touch with a British major named John André, who was chief intelligence officer to Sir Henry Clinton, the British general in occupied New York City. By the summer of 1779 André and Arnold were passing information through an elaborate spy network, possibly even using Peggy and her friends to pass secret notes back and forth. Arnold asked for money in exchange for information about troop movements and the location of various colonial supply depots. Clinton was happy to provide it, and the two began to negotiate a payment to reward Arnold for his treason.

By 1780 Arnold had fully committed to betraying his country. He began to sell property and transfer the money to Great Britain. That same year Arnold was made commander of the fort at West Point, New York. Today, West Point is the location of the United States Military Academy, but at the time it was an important part of the defense of the Hudson River. Occupying it would allow the British to divide the colonies in two.

General Clinton

Arnold began to systematically weaken the fort's defenses. He refused to order repairs to the fort, and he stationed soldiers in inefficient and unhelpful ways. In August 1780 he and Clinton came to an agreement. Arnold would let the British take the fort for £20,000.

In September 1780 André passed

West Point from Constitution Island

into American territory. He and Arnold had a meeting at the house of another British Loyalist. Arnold gave André a letter to take back to Clinton. He also gave André detailed drawings of West Point. But while traveling back to New York City, André was arrested, and his hidden papers were found. They were sent to General Washington. Washington quickly realized what they meant and gave orders for Arnold's arrest.

These orders came too late. Arnold heard of Andre's arrest, and he quickly arranged passage for himself into British-occupied territory. Once there, he wrote Washington a letter, asking that his wife, Peggy, be allowed to leave Philadelphia and join him in New York. Washington granted the request. Washington also tried to convince Clinton to trade Arnold for André, but Clinton refused the deal. After being found guilty by a military **tribunal**, André was hanged on October 2.

LATER LIFE

Arnold spent the remainder of the war fighting for the

The capture
of John André,
September 23, 1780

British. He led a force of soldiers that captured Richmond, Virginia, and then went on a rampage through the surrounding country. Later he and a small army of British soldiers seized and burned the town of New London, Connecticut. Legend has it that Arnold once asked a captured American soldier what would happen if the Americans captured Arnold. "They would cut off the leg that was wounded at Saratoga and bury it with the honors of war," was the reply. "The rest of you they would hang."

But Arnold's efforts, and the efforts of the British officers, proved useless. The British were outmaneuvered in the north, then defeated in the south. When Lord Charles Cornwallis surrendered with the remainder of the British army at Yorktown in 1781, it was clear that the war was over.

Arnold decided to move to Great Britain. He was given a substantial monetary reward, but the British public and government disliked him, and he had trouble finding work. While in London, Arnold discovered that traitors are universally hated, even by those who have bought their services.

In 1785 Arnold then moved to New Brunswick, Canada, where his family later joined him. There he started a shipping business, trading again with the West Indies. He quickly made himself unpopular in his new home as

Surrender of Cornwallis at Yorktown, 1781

well, so much so that at one point the townspeople burned a doll that looked like him. During one of his trips to the West Indies he was captured and briefly imprisoned by the French for spying. Arnold died in 1801 in London, a bitter and broken man.

Arnold's transformation from hero to traitor remains a source of fascination. Prior to his treason, he was a war hero, one of the few in the early stages of the American Revolution. His actions at Fort Ticonderoga and particularly at Saratoga showed great courage, as well as a clever military mind. Although by modern standards his desperate attempts to be promoted and recognized seem awfully crude, they were common at the time. Furthermore, it seems clear that Arnold had real reasons to be disappointed with his rewards. He was a skilled leader, but was passed over in favor of others who were less talented. Of course, none of this excuses his behavior. Greed, ambition, and bitterness motivated Arnold to betray his country. To this day, to call someone a "Benedict Arnold" is to accuse him of dishonesty and traitorous behavior.

BELLE BOYD

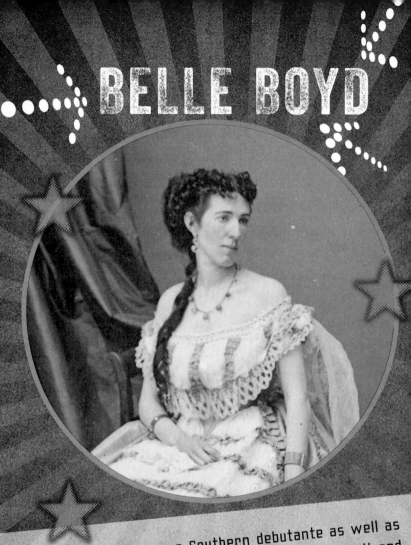

BELLE BOYD was a Southern debutante as well as a Confederate spy during the Civil War. Through wit and bravery, Boyd provided information to her hometown troops.

EARLY LIFE

The treasonous behavior of Benedict Arnold would have been unthinkable to Belle Boyd, also known as the "Cleopatra of the Secession" and "Siren of the Shenandoah." As a young woman in Virginia during the American Civil War, she risked her life and freedom to help her fellow Southerners. Along with her great personal sense of loyalty to the Confederacy, Boyd was also a regular thrill-seeker. Circumstances made her a spy. Her courage, which sometimes bordered on recklessness, made her a celebrity.

Isabella Marie "Belle" Boyd was born in May 1844 in what is now West Virginia. She was the eldest of eight children born to Benjamin and Mary Rebecca Boyd. The family was wealthy and owned slaves; her father ran a store. When Boyd was ten, she and her family moved to the town of Martinsburg, Virginia. She was carefree and something of a tomboy, playing with her brothers, climbing trees, and getting into fights.

Even as a child, Boyd was wild and rebellious. Her closest companion was her personal slave, Eliza Corsey, who would later assist Boyd in some of her adventures. As a child, Boyd taught Eliza to read. This was a serious crime in the South at this time. It was thought that learning to read would make slaves more likely to run away or rebel against their masters. The punishment for teaching a slave to read could be severe, but that did not seem to stop Boyd. But then, she didn't listen much to rules. Once when she was told she was too young to attend her parents' dinner party, she left and reentered the room on a horse. She looked at her astonished parents and said, "Well, my horse is old enough, isn't he?"

At twelve, Boyd left Martinsburg to attend Mount Washington Female College in Baltimore, Maryland. After graduating, Boyd went to Washington, DC, for her official coming-out party, which introduced her to society as a single woman of marriageable age. It seemed that Boyd's life, like that of many other Southern women, would be filled with social gatherings and dinner parties.

Mount Washington College

THE CIVIL WAR BEGINS

But life had other plans for young Boyd. After years of trying to compromise, the Northern free states and the Southern slave-owning states were at a crossroads. With the election of Abraham Lincoln in 1860, the Southern states determined that it was impossible to remain within the

President Abraham Lincoln

United States. They decided to **secede**, meaning that the eleven Southern states wanted to split from the United States and form their own country. It would be called the Confederate States of America, or the Confederacy for short. The leaders of the Southern states saw this as perfectly legal.

The Northern states, now called the Union, strongly disagreed. Both sides began to prepare for war. In the spring of 1861 Confederate forces attacked Fort Sumter, in South Carolina. The stage was set for what would become the bloodiest conflict in U.S. history, which would devastate the country and ultimately lead to more than 600,000 deaths and great suffering.

Like everyone else, Boyd was concerned and fearful about what the war would bring. Virginia was on the front

View of
Fort Sumt
1863

lines of the conflict and would remain so throughout the war. Martinsburg was located between the Union capital in Washington, DC, and the Confederate capital in Richmond, Virginia. Martinsburg and the rest of northern Virginia was a battleground for the next four years.

On July 4 Union forces under General Robert Patterson captured Martinsburg. His soldiers began to loot the town, going from house to house looking for liquor and valuable goods. Eventually, a small group of them came to Boyd's house. Boyd's father had already left to join the Confederate army, and thus the house was undefended.

The drunken soldiers tried to hang a Union flag over the doorway. Boyd's mother, Mary Boyd, stopped them, saying, "Men, every member of my household will die before that flag shall be raised over us." Angered, one of the soldiers threatened Mary Boyd. Belle Boyd, fearing for her mother's safety, pulled a small pistol from her pocket and shot the man dead.

General
Robert
Patterson

In most times and places, murdering the soldier of an occupying power would result in a quick death by hanging. But by the peculiar code of behavior followed at that time,

Confederate
flag

Boyd was innocent. The disrespect shown to Boyd and her mother, two women of property and reputation, justified Boyd's actions. A Union board of inquiry decided that Boyd's actions in defense of her mother and family were acceptable, and she was cleared of all wrongdoing.

"THE SIREN OF THE SHENANDOAH"

The disrespect shown by the Union soldiers and their occupation of her own beloved town infuriated Boyd. Her father, brothers, and other male relatives were all fighting in the Confederate army. Boyd decided that she would strike out against the Union in the only way she could—as a spy.

Northern Virginia was a center of spycraft during this period. As both sides in the war spoke the same language, often with the same accent, it was easy to pretend to be a supporter for the enemy. Neither the Union nor the Confederacy had anything like a professional spy service. The Union relied on a small group of private detectives called the Pinkerton Agency. Their spies were people who had opportunities to learn Confederate secrets and the bravery to pass them on.

Not only was Boyd cleared of any legal charges for shooting a Union soldier, but Union guards were stationed outside of her house. This was to keep Boyd and her family safe, and was also a sign of respect for her family. Boyd took advantage of being in close quarters with Union officers. She listened closely for any information that might help the Confederate cause. She also faked a romantic interest in some of the Union officers, the better to spy on them. Of one of these officers she later wrote, "I am indebted for some very remarkable effusions, some withered flowers, and last, not least, for a great deal of very important information, which was carefully transmitted to my countrymen."

Martinsburg was right on the edge of Union territory. Confederate troops were nearby, and Boyd came up with a variety of ways to send them the secrets she had gathered. She would also steal the personal weapons of Union soldiers and smuggle them to the Confederates, who were desperate for weapons at the time. Boyd also worked as a courier for Confederate Generals Thomas J. "Stonewall" Jackson and P. G. T. Beauregard. She would pass secret information back and forth between agents of the two generals.

It was while passing these letters that Boyd found herself once again in trouble with the Union. One of the notes that she had sent, but which she had not

Stonewall Jackson

P. G. T.
Beauregard

bothered to put into code, found its way into the hands of a Union captain. Boyd was summoned to appear before him. He warned her that her behavior was treason against the United States, and that punishment for treason was execution. But she was again released. The code of behavior at the time meant that it was difficult to punish a woman of Boyd's position. And the captain probably felt that Boyd's spying was more mischievous than anything else.

For a time, Boyd stopped her spying, though more because she was now busy with other work. After the Battle of Bull Run in July 1861, Boyd worked as a nurse at Front Royal, Virginia. It was becoming clear that the war would not be short or end easily. Boyd spent that winter in Martinsburg, which was now controlled by Confederate forces. The cold and bad weather meant that no major military operations were possible, but Boyd still managed to have one small adventure. Out riding one day, she traveled past the Confederate lines. Two Union officers met her and offered to ride her back into Confederate territory. When they returned to the Confederate lines, Boyd's allies, who had been waiting for her, ambushed and captured the Union officers.

It was another example of Boyd using etiquette to her advantage, something at which she was very good. She understood the customs of the time and relied on them when dealing with men from both armies. She herself, however, did not often bother to follow these customs. She concerned herself with doing whatever damage she could to the Union, even if she had to break her word at times. But honesty is generally not a virtue in a spy—nor is politeness!

THE DANGERS OF BEING A FAMOUS SPY

By the spring of 1862 Boyd had become something of a celebrity. Her daring behavior and clever tongue had made

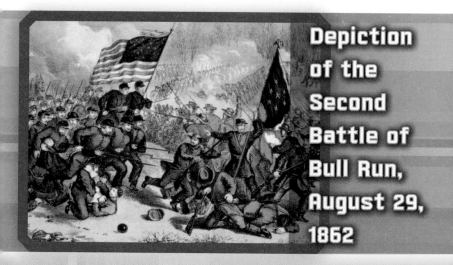

Depiction of the Second Battle of Bull Run, August 29, 1862

her famous in the South and an object of hatred in the North. Normally, being a celebrity and being a spy don't go well together. But Boyd continued as best she could. As a high-class Southern woman, she was able to mix socially with Union officers. But she was also brave and independent. She would sometimes dress up as a man or a poor servant girl to move back and forth across enemy lines.

During this time Boyd was briefly arrested and sent to Baltimore. Rather than imprison her, guards put her up at one of the most expensive hotels in the city. No one was exactly clear on what to do with Boyd. She could not be executed or easily imprisoned. After a week, she was released and returned to Front Royal.

Front Royal was once again on the front lines. The legendary Confederate General "Stonewall" Jackson was stationed just to the south. The Union army, led by General James Shields, was quartered in Front Royal itself. Everyone knew that Shields and the Union army were planning to attack, but no one knew the exact specifics.

No one besides Boyd, that is. After returning to Front Royal, she quickly returned to spying. One night she hid herself in a closet while Shields and his other officers discussed their battle plans. After eavesdropping on this secret conversation, Boyd dressed up as a man and slipped out into the night. After several missteps, she managed to get her information into the hands of a friend in Jackson's army.

But this was still not enough for Boyd. Just before the battle itself, she ran through the Union lines, dodging musket fire and artillery shells. She managed to find Jackson and tell him that the Union force was small; a direct attack would result in a victory. For her courage in providing this intelligence, she was given the Southern Cross of Honor. Later she was even made an honorary aide-de-camp.

The Confederates captured Front Royal but held it for only a week. When the Union army returned, Boyd was once again arrested, then once again released. Everyone knew that she was a spy, but they lacked concrete proof. Moreover, it was unclear what exactly could be done with Boyd after arresting her. The Union officers admired her courage and even the patriotism she had for the South. They didn't want to hang her or put her in prison.

Boyd continued her anti-Union activities, even right beneath the noses of the Northern army. But finally, her luck ran out. In Front Royal she met a man who claimed to be a Confederate soldier. Her slave, Eliza Corsey, insisted that she had seen the man associating with other Northerners, but Boyd did not believe her. In fact, Corsey was right. The man was a Union spy trying to trap Boyd. Boyd fell for a con that she herself had perfected. She gave the double agent a secret note to take to Jackson. Instead, the man took it to the Union war office.

This time Boyd did not escape prison. She was taken to Washington, DC, where she was put into the Old Capitol Prison. While there, Boyd was far from a perfect inmate. She complained often of her conditions and at one point got hold of a Confederate flag and hung it out of her window. After a month, she was released in a prisoner exchange, and took a ship to Richmond. There she met again with Jackson. He told her that it was best that she remain in Richmond, or even go farther south. The Union controlled her home of Martinsburg and if she returned and started her spying again, she would be arrested.

Boyd went for a time to Tennessee, then South Carolina, and then back to Richmond. She was beloved in the South for her courage in making trouble for the Union. Mobs of people would wait outside her hotel room to hear her speak about her adventures and her faith in the South's ultimate victory.

Although Boyd was much beloved for her work, her fame also made it impossible to continue being a spy. By now, she was too well-known to continue on as she had in the past. Also, years of brutal warfare had made the Union less

The Old Capitol Prison in Washington, DC

interested in **gallantry** and more interested in ensuring that spies went to jail.

In the spring of 1863, after a series of surprising victories in Virginia, the Confederates again pushed north. Martinsburg was once more within Confederate territory, and Boyd returned home. But after its crushing defeat at Gettysburg, Pennsylvania, the South quickly lost this territory. Boyd elected to remain in Martinsburg, despite the risk of imprisonment. It was a mistake. Boyd was again arrested and sent to Washington, DC. And once again, she made trouble. She would smuggle Confederate flags into the prison and hang them from her window, or sing

Belle Boyd

Confederate anthems loudly to annoy the prison guards.

Eventually Boyd was released. She made her way back to Richmond. But feeling miserable and unsure of what to do, she decided to travel to Europe. She was given some correspondence to take to England on behalf of the Confederate government. Taking a ship to England was not so easy to do. Confederate ships risked getting captured and boarded by the Union navy. This is exactly what happened to Boyd's ship. She was taken to New York City and kept there while the Union authorities decided whether to let her continue to London. Eventually they decided to let her go. She went from New York to Boston, from Boston to Montreal, and from Montreal to England.

LATER LIFE

While in England, Boyd got married. Amazingly, her new husband was Samuel Wylde Hardinge, the same Union naval officer who had arrested her a few months earlier! Their fairy-tale marriage did not last, however. Hardinge seems to have run off shortly after marrying Boyd, though the exact circumstances of his disappearance are unclear.

Stranded in England, poor, and carrying Hardinge's child, Boyd wrote and published a memoir of her time as a war spy, *Belle Boyd in Camp and Prison*. Though filled with exaggerations and half-truths, it became popular in England and back in the United States.

In 1865 the Civil War finally came to an end. It had been four years of ongoing struggle. To this day it remains the bloodiest war in American history. Boyd's beloved South was devastated. Many of her friends and family had died. The lifestyle that Boyd had enjoyed as a wealthy slave owner in Virginia was over forever.

But there was still strong sympathy for the Confederate

cause throughout the South, and Boyd was still a celebrity. She returned to the United States, where she went on speaking tours around the country. She would wear a Confederate uniform, carry dueling pistols, and act out scenes from her memoir. For a time Boyd enjoyed great popularity. She was so popular, in fact, that imitators pretended to be Boyd, hoping to make money off of the real Boyd's adventures!

Boyd married twice more: first to John Swainston Hammond, an English businessman, and then to Nathaniel Rue High, an actor from Ohio. She continued to perform portions of her life story onstage. But in time her popularity faded and she struggled to make ends meet. People were less interested in the Civil War and questioned the accuracy of Boyd's story. Toward the end of her life, she wrote, "Fortune has played me a sad trick by letting me live on and on."

Boyd was on a speaking tour in Wisconsin when she died of a heart attack on June 11, 1900. She was scheduled to give a lecture to members of the Grand Army of the Republic, a Union veterans' association. She was fifty-six years old. She had outlived her beloved Confederacy by thirty-five years.

Boyd was a spy for a country that only existed briefly and never had a formal spy service. Despite her bravery and cleverness, the intelligence she gathered for the

Confederacy did little to impact the war. Her career as a spy was relatively short. Sudden fame made it impossible to continue as a spy. But she stands out as a person of extraordinary courage and cleverness, who did her best to serve a cause she thought noble.

VIRGINIA HALL

VIRGINIA HALL is known as one of the most famous spies of World War II. Despite losing one leg years prior, the Nazis considered her to be extremely dangerous and America considered her incredibly valuable.

EARLY LIFE

The reality of spycraft is often far less interesting than how it is portrayed in films and on television. It is more about long nights looking over paperwork than narrow escapes from the enemy. In the case of Virginia Hall, however, the reality actually lives up to the myth. Fearless, clever, and tough as nails, Hall went from privileged socialite to the woman the Nazi **Gestapo** called "the most dangerous Allied spy." During the course of World War II she ran a deep **covert** operation behind enemy lines, spying on the Nazis and saving the lives of pilots shot down over Nazi-occupied territory. And she did it all while hobbling around on one leg!

Hall was born in Baltimore on April 6, 1906. Her family was wealthy and well-connected. She therefore had more opportunities than most women at the time. She studied at Radcliffe College in Massachusetts and Barnard College in New York City. She learned foreign languages and could speak in French, German, and Italian. With the assistance of her family, she spent long periods of time traveling in Europe. Her familiarity with the continent and her understanding of its people would be immeasurably helpful when she began working as a spy some years later.

After leaving college, Hall wanted to live and work abroad. She got a job as a clerk in the Consular Service at the American Embassy in Warsaw, Poland. She had hopes of joining the U.S. Foreign Service, and working at an embassy was a good first step. With her intelligence, foreign-language ability, and drive, it seemed there would be no limit to what Hall could accomplish.

But then tragedy struck. While on a hunting trip in Turkey, Hall accidentally shot herself in the leg. The injury was a very bad one. The bottom half of the injured leg required amputation. It was removed below the knee and replaced with a wooden limb. In a show of the spirit that defined her character, Hall nicknamed the new wooden leg "Cuthbert." It went on to play a **prominent** role in her legend.

Hall's hope of joining the Foreign Service was an ambitious one. Although it was not technically against the rules for women to work there, very few were allowed to at that point. With her leg injured, it was impossible for her to ever rise to the position she hoped to fill, due to a requirement that individuals in the Foreign Service possess all their limbs. Bored and depressed, she resigned from the State Department in 1939, but remained in Europe.

By this time, Germany had come out of World War I a bankrupt and broken nation, forced to pay huge amounts of money in war **reparations** to the victorious nations of France and Great Britain. But it was making a comeback under a dictator, Adolf Hitler. In 1939 Germany launched an unprovoked war against the nation of Czechoslovakia. France and Great Britain looked on helplessly. Believing that they would never stand up against his ambitions, Hitler went on to invade Poland later that year. This was too much for the British and French to accept, and the two nations declared war on Germany.

Adolf Hitler

The United States initially remained neutral in the conflict, believing that the war in Europe was not their concern. Hall, however, believed differently. She was living in Paris when war broke out, and she signed up to work as an ambulance driver. Her skills were put to good use when Germany, in a lightning-fast strike in the spring of 1940, steamrolled its way through France. Hall showed great courage in her time as an ambulance driver, taking the sick and seriously wounded to receive treatment while facing enemy fire.

The French army was unprepared for the speed and
ferociousness of the German attack and suffered many
casualties. When the fighting stopped in the summer of
1940, France was forced to agree to a humiliating series
of terms. A new French government was put in place, the
so-called Vichy government. Vichy France was essentially a
puppet state of Germany, willing to do whatever the Nazis
wanted.

THE "LIMPING WOMAN" FIGHTS THE NAZIS

The French may have given up the fight, but Hall would
keep on fighting. For her, the war had just begun. As a
citizen with a passport from a neutral country, she was able
to leave France. Not sure of what to do, she made her way to
England. While at a dinner party she met a woman named
Vera Atkins, who was secretly a member of the Special
Operations Executive. The SOE was the British spy agency
responsible for planning and carrying out acts of spycraft
and sabotage within German-occupied areas. Although
born in Romania and not technically even a British citizen,
Atkins had become a member of the SOE because of her
intelligence, bravery, and deep network of contacts. Atkins
worked in "F" section, the branch of the SOE that operated
in France.

Finding people with the skills and bravery necessary

to enter occupied France and work there on behalf of the British government was a constant struggle. Atkins found an ideal foreign agent in Hall. Hall knew many foreign languages, had spent long years living in Europe, and had extensive contacts in France. Most importantly, she was brave enough to accept the job! Anxious to do her part to fight against Hitler, Hall signed up with the SOE. She became the SOE's first female operative and was trained in the many skills required of a foreign spy. Hall learned how to operate a resistance group, pass coded messages, use small arms, and many other skills.

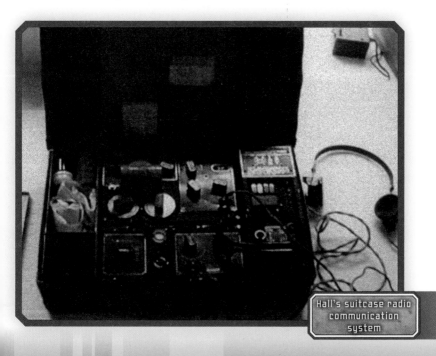

Hall's suitcase radio communication system

After this period of training, Hall returned to France, arriving on August 23, 1941. First she had to register in Vichy, the capital of occupied France. Then she traveled to the city of Lyon, which was a **hotbed** of resistance against the Germans. Her cover was as a reporter for the *New York Post*. But in reality she was there to coordinate actions of the many British and Free French agents working in France at that time. She operated under any number of different aliases—that is, false names and identities—calling herself Bridgette LeContre, Marie, Philomène, and Germaine. She passed money from the SOE home office to various agents, and information from the agents back to the office. On several occasions she also helped to smuggle downed British airmen across the English Channel and back to their country. All the while she kept up her cover as a newspaper reporter, writing articles that were published back in the United States.

Hall's position was incredibly dangerous. As a foreign agent, she would be executed if captured by the Germans, and likely tortured first. Beyond all the many normal difficulties of a person in her position, Hall's life was even more complicated because she was a woman. Many men in the French Resistance didn't think a woman could be tough or smart enough to hold such an important wartime position. Ultimately, Hall's competence and bravery won them over. She was daring, clever, and willing to attempt missions that no one else would have. In one of her many extraordinary adventures, Hall managed to rescue two comrades who had been captured and were being held in a Gestapo prison.

Hall spent fourteen months working deep undercover, doing her best to throw a wrench in the German war machine. Over time, the Germans became aware of her existence, though they never learned the names she operated under or her exact location. The Gestapo, the dreaded and hated secret police, put out a wanted notice in

The head of the Nazi German SS and Gestapo, Heinrich Himmler inspects a German prisoner of war.

hopes of capturing her. It read:

"The woman who limps is one of the most dangerous Allied agents in France. We must find and destroy her."

During her time in Lyon, the international situation changed. Germany's swift victory over France was the last Nazi win. Despite a long campaign of intense bombing, it was unable to knock Britain out of the war. Hitler, paranoid about the possibility that the Soviet Union would join the war unexpectedly, decided on a surprise attack. Though the Nazis enjoyed early success, their army got bogged down in

The USS *Arizona* burning at Pearl Harbor, Dec. 7, 19

the vastness of western Soviet Union. Meanwhile, Japan, an ally of Germany, made a surprise attack on the United States at Pearl Harbor, hoping to cripple its ability to fight a war in the Pacific Ocean. It had the opposite effect, infuriating the U.S. public and bringing the nation into the war on the Allied side. In November 1942 the Americans and British launched Operation Torch, an invasion of French-controlled territory in North Africa. Fearing that the weak Vichy regime would not put up a fight against its former allies, the Germans officially took over the rest of France.

Hall's position had suddenly become even more dangerous. The United States was no longer a neutral power, and the Gestapo would be looking for her even more furiously than before. She needed to escape France, but there was no easy way out. She decided to make her way from Lyon, in the central east of France, south across the Pyrenees mountains and into Spain. Winter comes early in the high Pyrenees mountaintops, and Hall was forced to cross on her feet—or foot, in Hall's case! But she survived the dangerous journey. It was an extraordinary adventure in its own right, but it was just one of Hall's many incredible accomplishments.

Before fleeing occupied France, Hall sent a secret telegraph message to the SOE central office, warning

An artist's rendering of Hall transmitting messages from occupied France using her suitcase radio

that she might have difficulty escaping because of "Cuthbert." She meant that she anticipated trouble in walking from France to Spain because she didn't have two legs to walk with! The SOE agent, however, was unfamiliar with the nickname Hall had given her wooden leg. Thinking Cuthbert was another agent who worked for Hall, the SOE agent wired back, "If Cuthbert troublesome, eliminate him!"

ONCE MORE INTO THE BREACH

Hall had escaped from France in the nick of time, but she wasn't out of trouble yet. The Spanish were suspicious of this strange one-legged American woman who spoke French and walked across mountains in the winter. She was imprisoned for several weeks, but was ultimately allowed to leave prison.

For most people, spending a year and a half as a spy in Nazi territory would be enough adventure to last a lifetime. But Hall was not most people. She immediately requested that the SOE send her back to France to continue her work there. The SOE refused. Hall was too well-known in France to be an effective agent. Her wanted poster circulated everywhere. The Germans were well aware of the "limping lady" and what a threat she was to them.

Instead, Hall ended up working for the SOE in Madrid. It was important work, but far from the excitement of the

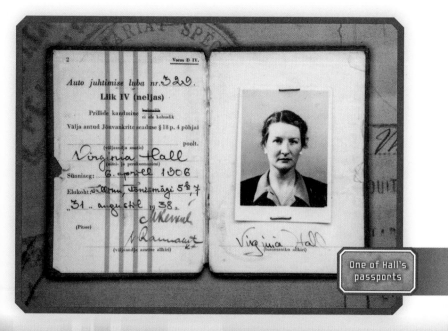

One of Hall's passports

King George VI presented Hall with the Order of the British Empire Medal in 1943 for her undercover work in France.

deep-cover operations that Hall had been involved with in France. She found it very dull, and after a year requested an assignment with more danger and excitement.

Hall returned to London. Recognizing her extraordinary service, Great Britain granted her the Order of the British Empire, an honor given to those who have done great service for the country. Still, the SOE refused to send her back into occupied territory.

But Hall's exploits were far from over. In 1944 the U.S. and British forces were preparing to retake France from Germany. It would be the largest seaborne invasion ever attempted. If it succeeded, the Allies would have a foothold on the continent to take the fight straight to Germany. Failure, however, would mean disaster.

But before the invasion itself, the Allies began to send spies over to France to prepare the way. Hall was given the job of briefing these agents on what they could expect in France. There were few people more qualified to do so, and the job was an important one. But Hall still craved excitement and danger. She didn't want to be training spies to be sent to France; she wanted to be sent to France herself. With the hope of making it more likely that she would be sent back, she trained as a radio operator, a crucial specialty for spies working in enemy territory. Still the SOE thought Hall was too well-known in France to be able to run an intelligence operation.

While she was in London working for the SOE, Hall made contacts with the recently created Office of Strategic Services. The OSS was the U.S. equivalent of the SOE, essentially the U.S. spy service. After the war it would become the Central Intelligence Agency, or the CIA. Hall had not been paying much attention to this upstart organization run by her countrymen, but she saw an opportunity to return to active service. Hall approached some of her contacts in the OSS and convinced them to send her back across the English Channel, to be part of a network of spies and **saboteurs** code-named "Saint."

In the spring of 1944 Hall was on a motorboat speeding across the Channel. Many agents were parachuted in, but this was impossible because of Hall's wooden leg. She was dressed as an elderly farmhand and was dropped ashore in the dead of night. Hall quickly got back to what she did best: making trouble for the Nazis. As the U.S. and Allied forces marched their way east toward Germany, Hall acquired intelligence on enemy movements and used her radio skills to help the Resistance. She transported ammunition and weapon drops from the Royal Air Force to members of the Free French.

Hall also played an important role in Operation Jedburgh. Operation Jedburgh was a joint SOE-OSS operation meant to cause trouble for the Nazis before the actual invasion. Three-man groups consisting of two U.S. or British agents and one French agent were air-dropped into occupied France just before the landings at Normandy. Their goal was to meet up with members of the Resistance, provide them with ammunition and weapons, and sabotage the Nazis and to engage in **guerrilla** warfare. Hall worked with one of these Jedburgh groups to identify likely targets for sabotage or attack.

Astonishingly, as busy as she was during this period, Hall still found time for romance. One of the men in a Jedburgh group she was working with was named Paul Goillot. Goillot was a native Frenchman who had spent most of his life in New York City and returned to Europe to fight the Nazis. The two fell in love and would be married years later, after the war was over.

Allied forces had advanced to meet Hall in France, and her services with the Resistance were no longer needed. She trained with an OSS group to enter occupied Vienna, but the war ended before the operation was ever put into practice. When the OSS was **dismantled** shortly after Germany's

Hall and Paul Goillot (far right)

surrender, Hall stayed in Europe and joined the follow-up to the OSS, the Central Intelligence Group (later renamed the Central Intelligence Agency). She entered the clandestine wing of the service in 1947. In 1950 she and Goillot married.

LATER LIFE

In 1945 Hall was awarded a Distinguished Service Cross, the second-highest military award given by the United States. Hall was the only woman to receive one for her efforts during World War II. President Truman requested

Hall receiving the Distinguished Service Cross, 1945

that it be given to her in a public ceremony. But Hall refused, knowing that doing so would make it more difficult for her to work as a secret agent later on.

Though Hall never again worked as an undercover agent, she spent the rest of her professional life working as a CIA analyst, until her mandatory retirement at the age of sixty. Hall found the work less interesting than fighting Nazis in occupied France, and she thought that her gender made it more difficult to receive the assignments for which she felt capable. All the same, she was a dedicated and competent worker.

After finishing her service, Hall retired to a country home near Baltimore, where she was born. Even later in life, Hall was reluctant to talk about her experiences. When asked about her extraordinary wartime heroism, she would answer, "Many of my friends were killed for talking too much." Hall passed away quietly on July 12, 1982, at the age of seventy-six.

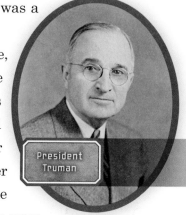

President Truman

Hall's is a story of almost unbelievable bravery and accomplishment. With nothing more than her natural courage, quickness of thought, and language skills, she survived for years in occupied territory, all while doing her best to defeat the Nazis. Hall is a perfect example of that peculiar character type that is drawn to clandestine work. She was never as happy as when her life was in danger. No escape was too narrow for her. As soon as she was safe, she immediately wanted to go back into danger.

ALLEN DULLES

ALLEN DULLES was the Director of the CIA from 1953-1961. During his service Dulles helped define modern espionage and became one of the most famous spies in history.

EARLY LIFE

There is perhaps no more important spy in the history of American intelligence than Allen Welsh Dulles. From his years fighting the rise of Nazi Germany to his work against the Soviet Union during the Cold War, he was probably the single most influential individual in the creation of the modern Central Intelligence Agency. He remains the longest-serving director of the CIA, and did much to **penetrate** the security of the Soviet Union. He set up valuable intelligence rings throughout Eastern Europe and the Communist world, and paved the way for future generations of CIA leaders.

Dulles was born in April 7, 1893, in Watertown, New York. He came from a family with deep and long-standing ties to government. A grandfather and uncle had both served as secretary of state for previous presidents, and his own brother, John Foster Dulles, would one day serve with great distinction as secretary of state for President Dwight D. Eisenhower's administration. After graduating from Princeton University

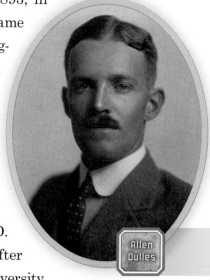

Allen Dulles

Princeton
University,
c. 1903

in 1916, Dulles entered the diplomatic service, moving to Switzerland to work in Bern. In 1920 he married Clover Todd. They had one son, Allen Macy Dulles. Dulles spent several years working in the diplomatic service, leaving to attend law school at George Washington University. After graduation in 1926, he worked at a major New York law firm, where his older brother, John Dulles, was a partner. But he continued playing an active role in foreign affairs, becoming a director of the Council on Foreign Relations.

Dulles came from a family that took foreign affairs very seriously, but this was not the case for all of the United States. Many Americans during this period were staunchly isolationist, meaning that they believed the United States should not play an active role in the politics of other countries. This attitude had strengthened after World War I and remained popular until the United States entered World War II. Many Americans believed that they had been tricked into entering World War I, and were understandably reluctant to get involved in a second war with Germany.

Dulles saw the situation more clearly. In 1935, he returned from a business trip to Berlin horrified by Germany's treatment of its Jewish population and committed to doing something about it. He convinced the other members of his

Dulles, 1924

law firm to close their branch in Berlin and to stop doing business with Germany. It was a brave stance, and one that relatively few people were willing to take during this period.

Dulles became an important voice arguing that America should adopt an active foreign policy. In 1938 he ran unsuccessfully for Congress on a platform of increased intervention in Europe. He also co-authored two books during this time, *Can We Be Neutral?* and *Can America Stay Neutral?,* which both argued that the shifting international scene meant that the United States could no longer remain neutral. Dulles also did what he could as a private citizen to help the German Jews, assisting several in escaping from Nazi territory.

WORLD WAR II

History would prove Dulles right. By the late 1930s it was clear that the European war everyone feared would come soon. At first the United States tried to remain neutral, even while the Axis powers—Germany, Italy, and Japan— went to war against the Allied nations of France and Great Britain. But as Japan's desire to expand in the Pacific Ocean began to interfere with U.S. interests in the region, it seemed increasingly likely that the United States would soon be drawn into the war. After the shocking attack on

Pearl Harbor attack, 1941

Pearl Harbor in December 1941, the United States had no choice but to go to war against Japan. Four days later, Germany declared war on the United States. Americans once again found themselves fighting on European soil.

With his history in the diplomatic service and early recognition of the Nazi threat, Dulles was an ideal choice for a spymaster. There was one problem: At this point, the United States did not have an intelligence agency. That changed when President Franklin D. Roosevelt ordered the creation of the Office of Strategic Services in 1942.

Roosevelt chose William Joseph Donovan, also known as "Wild Bill," to run it. Wild Bill was a World War I hero with a long history of intelligence work. He asked his friend Dulles to work for him to fight the Nazis.

Although Donovan wanted Dulles to work in the London office, Dulles felt he could be of more use in neutral Switzerland, since it bordered Germany. Dulles returned to Bern on November 9, 1942.

President Roosevelt

He only barely made it, catching a train from France just moments before the Nazis closed the border. Over the course of the next three years, Dulles worked tirelessly to gather information about the Nazis and support the resistance movements in occupied Europe. Among his many accomplishments during this period was making contact with a small group of high-ranking German army officers who were plotting to assassinate Adolf Hitler. Though the plot ultimately failed and the **conspirators** were executed, they passed Dulles early information about Germany's development of the V1 and V2 rockets, the secret weapons that Germany hoped would win the war. Dulles also was

A V2 rocket test at the White Sands Proving Ground in Las Cruces, New Mexico, 1946

responsible for negotiating an early peace with the German forces in Italy.

CIA DIRECTOR

After the war ended in 1945, Dulles left the OSS and returned to his work as a lawyer, though he did not remain in private life for long. The terrible destruction of World War II had shifted global politics. The once-great powers of France and Germany were greatly weakened and Germany was split in two: West Germany, a democracy backed by the United States, and East Germany, a Communist country

A German wall to a Jewish ghetto in Warsaw, Poland, 1940

receiving aid from the Soviet Union. There once had been many important international powers, but now the world, like Germany, seemed split in two. The United States and its allies faced the Soviet Union and its puppet countries, and these two new superpowers seemed ready to collide.

It was clear that the United States could not return to its isolationist policy. With the signing of the National Security Act of 1947, President Harry Truman created the Central Intelligence Agency, the follow-up to the OSS. Dulles was intimately involved in the creation of the CIA, serving on a three-member board that helped define the powers and purpose of the organization. In 1951 he was named deputy director of the new agency, and in 1953 he took over as head of the CIA.

The years that Dulles served as CIA director saw some of the agency's biggest victories, as well as its most glaring failures. The great challenge facing the agency at that time was the rivalry with the Soviet Union. In Europe, South America, East Asia, and Africa, each side worked to make sure that its allies remained in power and its enemies defeated. This was called the Cold War, and it dominated American political thought until the collapse of the Soviet Union in 1991.

But that collapse was a long way in the future. When Dulles took office, the Soviet Union seemed to be getting stronger, and Dulles threw everything he could into weakening it and limiting

President Truman

Dulles as CIA director

its power. He set up rings of spies in Eastern Europe. He worked to discover the spies that were already operating in the West, and to convert or capture them once they were discovered.

Like the Soviets, the CIA was constantly involved in putting out propaganda, information and news presented with a particular bias or slant. After becoming director of the CIA, Dulles was in charge of a program called Operation Mockingbird. Operation Mockingbird was a large, secret propaganda exercise where foreign and American reporters were bribed to write pro-American articles and put out pro-American information. During its height, Operation Mockingbird was tremendously effective, putting out propaganda that Dulles thought helped the United States and hurt the Soviets.

Dulles played a prominent role in the development of the U-2 spy plane. Unique at the time, it was an aircraft capable of flying extremely high and at extraordinary speeds while taking detailed photos of the ground below. It gave the United States an edge against the Soviets and was responsible for gathering much useful intelligence—until

U-2 spy plane with
NASA markings,
California, 1960

one crashed over Soviet territory, giving them the chance to inspect and copy the technology.

REGIME CHANGE

Dulles and other leaders at the time felt that it was not enough just to spy on the Soviet Union. They needed to make sure that American allies were in charge in other parts of the world. This belief led Dulles to two of his most controversial projects: the overthrow of the democratically elected prime minister of Iran in 1953 and the overthrow of the president of Guatemala a year later.

The Middle Eastern nation of Iran was rich in oil but not much else. Years earlier, when Iran was still a part of the

British Prime Minister
Clement Richard
Attlee, 1950

Shah of Iran, Reza
Pahlavi Mohammed,
c. 1950

British Empire, it had sold the rights to pump its oil to the Anglo-Iranian Oil Company. Over time, this British company had become extremely unpopular among Iranians, who perceived it as stealing Iran's natural wealth. In 1951, the prime minister of Iran nationalized the oil, which stripped the Anglo-Iranian Oil Company of the right to pump oil and gave it back to the Iranian government. The British were furious because the Anglo-Iranian Oil Company was one of their most profitable assets. Great Britain discussed this with the United States, which decided to put its backing behind the shah of Iran. The shah was essentially the king of Iran, though like the queen of Great Britain, he had very little actual power. The CIA bribed

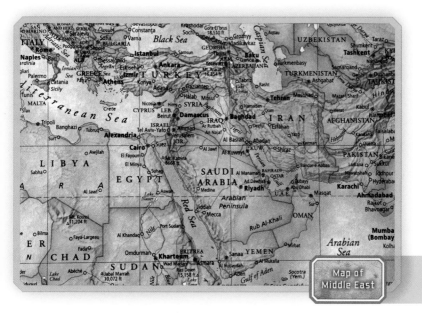

Map of Middle East

military and civil leaders to support the shah. The prime minister was overthrown, and the shah became the head of the government.

The United States' reasons for taking part in this operation are still up for debate. There was some fear that the Iranian government might swing into the Soviet orbit. Eisenhower, Dulles, and other leaders probably preferred a weak, pro-American leader like the shah to the leftist, possibly anti-American leaders that were in place at the time. It was also the case that under the shah the United States had access to the tremendously valuable Iranian oil fields.

A year later and halfway across the world, a similar situation played out. In the 1950s the United Fruit Company, a U.S. importer that grew and sold fruit, was one of the major political players in South America. In Guatemala in particular, it owned a tremendous amount of land. United Fruit also had powerful friends in the U.S. government—like Dulles, who had served on the company's board of trustees.

So in the early 1950s when President Jacobo Árbenz Guzmán began to nationalize some of the land that United Fruit claimed as its own, the company leaders knew who to talk to. With the support of Eisenhower, Dulles and the CIA provided weapons, money, and training to right-wing opponents of Guzmán. Aided by the CIA and the U.S. military, the right-wing militia invaded Guatemala from its base in Nicaragua. The invasion itself soon ran into difficulties. But the knowledge that the mighty United States was actively against Guzmán convinced the leaders of the Guatemalan army to give up.

President Jacobo Arbenz Guzmán, Switzerland, c. 1955

Though successful in the short

term, in the long term the interventions in Iran and Guatemala proved to be something close to disasters. The government Dulles installed in Guatemala did not last long: President Castillo Armas was assassinated in 1957. Afterward, Guatemala collapsed into an incredibly violent and long-lasting civil war, which would devastate the country for decades. It was never clear that Guzmán was actually a Communist, or that Guatemala had a real role to play in the Cold War.

In Iran the shah was massively unpopular, seen by his people as an American puppet uninterested in their well-being. His regime was so brutal, and he himself so weak and incompetent, that he was eventually overthrown in 1979. The regime that replaced him turned out to be similarly corrupt, while also being intensely anti-American. Dulles solved a small problem in the present, but created a much bigger one for the United States years down the line.

DOWNFALL

At the time, however, Dulles was looking good. At a relatively small cost, he was able to overthrow two regimes in faraway parts of the world that were seen as hostile to the United States. Then he was able to replace them with leaders who were thought to be pro-American. With this experience as a guide, when the small island country of

Cuba was taken over by the **Communist** forces of Fidel Castro in 1959, Dulles thought he knew exactly what to do.

Unlike in Iran and Guatemala, there were good reasons for being concerned about the government of Castro. Castro was openly a Communist and received money and training from the Soviet Union. Enemies of the regime were fired from their jobs, forced from their houses, and sometimes even executed. The fact that Cuba is only ninety miles from the United States was another serious concern. Cuba offered the Soviet Union a platform from which it could attack the United States, either as a launching pad for a direct invasion or a base to put missiles.

Shortly before leaving office, Eisenhower directed Dulles to create Operation 40, a group of agents who concentrated on finding ways to eliminate or overthrow the Communist regime in Cuba. Much information regarding the CIA's activities during this period remains cloaked in mystery. However, it seems clear that the CIA reached out to various sources to try to assassinate Fidel Castro and other Communist leaders. They also attempted acts of sabotage within Cuba itself, but none were particularly successful.

Dulles and others within the CIA decided the time had come to do in Cuba what they had done in Guatemala six years before. They would find and train an army, and use it to overthrow Castro. The CIA made contact with Cuban

Fidel Castro, 1959

refugees living in Florida, men who had escaped from Cuba to avoid persecution and wanted to free their homeland. The CIA gave them special training in guerilla combat and jungle warfare. It also provided them with American equipment. At first, Dulles hoped to send the men in by parachute. When that proved impossible, the United States decided to invade by sea. John F. Kennedy became president in 1961, in part because of his strong anti-Communist, anti-Castro platform. He told Dulles to go ahead with the plan, which was already well under way.

On April 17, 1961, the anti-Castro forces landed at the

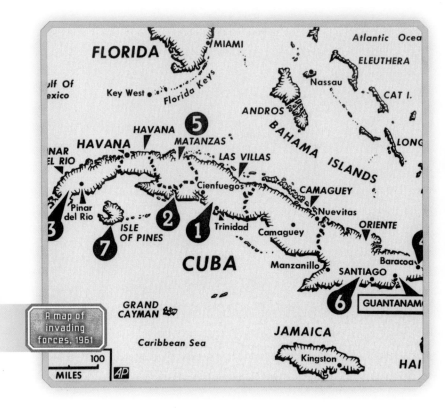

A map of invading forces, 1961

Bay of Pigs in the south of Cuba. After that, everything went wrong. The Soviet spy system had discovered the plan and informed Castro. Castro's army was far larger and much better trained than the American-backed forces. The battle was over quickly and most of the rebels were captured. Castro later ransomed them for millions of dollars.

It was a humiliating failure for Dulles and the United

States. Within Latin America, the Bay of Pigs fiasco made the United States immensely unpopular. The country looked like a bully that thought it could intervene anywhere it wanted to in the region. More importantly, it made the United States seem weak and incompetent. The Soviets were furious at the attack, and relations between the Soviet Union and the United States became even more tense. The Bay of Pigs fiasco, and CIA involvement in Cuba, would lead to the Cuban Missile Crisis a year later.

Although Kennedy had backed the plan, he was furious that he had been embarrassed so early in his presidency.

JFK and Dulles, c. 1961

He felt that Dulles and others in the CIA misled him. Dulles had to go. In September 1961 Dulles and his staff were forced to resign.

In Dulles's mind, the attempted invasion of Cuba, like the operations in Iran and Guatemala, was crucial to protect the United States. He believed that the Cold War between the United States and the Soviet Union demanded that pro-American leaders be put in charge of foreign countries. Having a Soviet-aligned leader in Tehran, Iran, or Havana, Cuba, gave the Soviet Union an ally in the fight against the United States. Overthrowing them was necessary, even if some of the activities Dulles took part in were against U.S. law. As long as these interventions were successful, Americans mostly agreed with Dulles. The interventions in Iran and Guatemala were generally accepted by the United States public, largely because the CIA used propaganda to shape public opinion. It was mainly because the United States as a whole was very worried about the Soviet Union's growing strength.

Allen
Dulles,
1966

LATER YEARS AND DEATH

Dulles retired to private life after leaving the CIA. He published a book called *The Craft of Intelligence* in 1963. But history was not quite done with him. After Kennedy's assassination, Dulles was chosen to sit on the Warren Commission. The Warren Commission was created by

President Lyndon B. Johnson

Warren Commission, 1964

CIA head
Allen Dulles,
1960

President Lyndon Johnson to investigate the circumstances behind Kennedy's death. Dulles and the other members of the commission ultimately decided that Kennedy's assassination was the work of a single gunman, though there are many conspiracy theories that argue otherwise.

Dulles died of pneumonia in 1969, in Washington, DC. His time as CIA director remains controversial, particularly his interventions in Iran and Guatemala. Some see him as a heroic man working in extraordinarily difficult circumstances. They believe that the success he had spying on the Soviets was essential to the United

States' ultimate victory in the Cold War. Others argue that he and the CIA did more harm than good, getting involved in unimportant areas of the world for unclear reasons. Still, in his many years as a spy—first fighting against the Nazis, then against the Soviets—Dulles set the standard for what an American spy could be.

KIM PHILBY

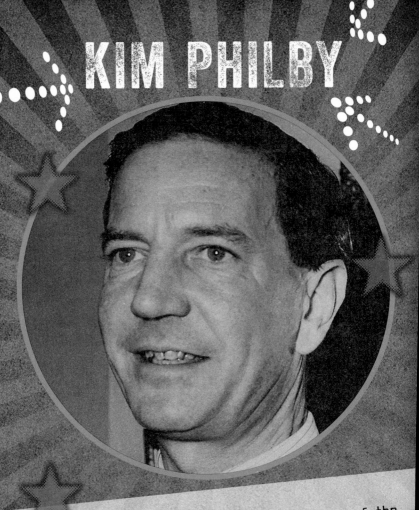

KIM PHILBY was a high-ranking member of the British intelligence service during the Cold War. All the while, he worked as a double agent for the Soviet Union, and was a member of a spy ring called the Cambridge Five.

YOUTH

The end of World War II brought with it a **professionalization** of the spy services, as well as a new mission. For most of the twentieth century, the two new superpowers—the capitalist West, led by the United States, and the Communist East, led by the Soviet Union—found themselves locked in a high-stakes game of espionage and counterespionage. Spycraft was elevated to a new level, made far more elaborate and complex. Billions of dollars were spent by both sides on training, developing foreign spies, and technology. Of all the many spies working at that time, there was probably no single agent who found more success than Kim Philby. He was one of the most powerful men in the British spy service—despite the fact that he was working secretly for the Soviets!

He was born Harold Adrian Russell Philby in India on January 1, 1912. His father, Harry Saint John Philby, worked for the Indian Civil Service, a branch of the British government that governed India. After converting to Islam, Philby's father became an influential adviser for the king of Saudi Arabia. His son was nicknamed Kim early in life, after the hero of the Rudyard Kipling novel of that name. As the child of a prominent and well-connected British gentleman, young Philby's life was well planned. He went to Westminster School and then Cambridge University,

Kim and the letter writer: illustration from Rudyard Kipling's novel *Kim*

where he graduated with an economics degree in 1933.

It was during his time as a student at Cambridge that Philby took his first steps on the road toward becoming a Communist agent. Communism is a political philosophy that was founded by Karl Marx and Friedrich Engels in 1848. It argues that the system of national governments should be overthrown and replaced by an international system of government run by representatives of the working class. Once this revolution occurred, all of the great problems of the world—war, famine, poverty—would disappear. Although the reality of Communism proved to be very different, the dream it offered excited several generations of men and women throughout the world. When the Russian Empire collapsed after its defeat in World War I, it was replaced by the Soviet Union, a government that was theoretically organized around the Communist

Map of
Soviet Union

belief system. Many young men and women saw the Soviet Union as a hope for a better world, and betrayed their countries for it.

Philby was one of these people. An enthusiastic Communist, Philby joined the World Committee for the Relief of the Victims of German Fascism, which was one of many organizations that were actually a cover for the Soviet spies. Two other students, Donald Maclean and Guy Burgess, were recruited around the same time, and

The "Cambridge Three,"
Donald Duart Maclean,
Kim Philby, and Guy Burgess

also went on to provide the Soviets with inside information from the British intelligence services. Philby, Maclean, and Burgess would go down in history as the so-called "Cambridge Three."

WORKING FOR THE SOVIETS

After graduation, Philby went to Vienna, where he worked to aid the victims of the Nazi terror. While there he met Litzi Friedmann, an Austrian-Hungarian Jew and a devoted Communist. Although it is unclear exactly when Philby went from being politically affiliated with Communism to being a full-fledged Soviet agent, it seems likely that Friedmann played a role in converting him. The two married in 1934. As the political situation in Austria declined, Philby and Friedmann fled to London.

In London, Philby studied Slavic languages and worked

to develop contacts within the German community, pretending he was a Nazi sympathizer in an effort to gain information for his Soviet masters. Also around this time Philby and Friedmann broke up, though they did not officially divorce until 1946.

In 1937, Philby traveled to Spain. At this point Spain was in the middle of a violent civil war between the Communist-backed Republican armies and the **Fascist** forces of Francisco Franco. In many ways, the Spanish Civil War was a training ground for World War II. The Republicans were given money and training by the Soviets, while Nazi Germany lent weapons and men to the Fascists. Many young **idealists** from across Europe and the world traveled to Spain to take part in the conflict.

Philby's cover was as a freelance journalist, though he was secretly passing information to both the British and the Soviets. At one point he was a part of a Soviet plot to assassinate Franco, but the plan fizzled out without an attempt on the general's life. In fact, Philby's pro-Franco writings, and a minor wound he suffered at the hands of a Republican artillery shell, made him something of a hero to Franco's supporters. The Fascists even gave him a medal!

Philby returned to London in 1939. He seems to have become conflicted about Communism by this point, and he stopped meeting with his Soviet handler, a term meaning the person responsible for passing information and orders between a spy and the country he is spying for. Around this time he met Aileen Furse, whom he later married. After a chance meeting with a British intelligence operative, Philby was offered a position in the War Office. While there, he came back into contact with his old college friend Burgess, still a Communist agent.

Philby was put in charge of training counterintelligence operatives for the Secret Intelligence Service (also known as MI6), the branch of the British government responsible for foreign spying. At first he was in charge of operations around Spain and Portugal, but soon he was put in charge of operations in Italy and North Africa as well. Again, he passed information to the Soviets. Most of it involved information he had gained as a British agent about Nazi Germany's war plans, and some of it proved critical to the Soviet Union when Germany declared war on it in 1941.

It is part of the nature of intelligence work that it is ultimately impossible for any country to entirely trust its spies. For all the information Philby provided them, the Soviets never stopped being suspicious that he was working for the British all along, passing information only when it served British interests. Though willing to provide information regarding German activities, Philby seemed slow to give any insight into the spying activities against the Soviet Union itself. The belief that Philby was a double agent, only pretending to work for the Soviets, was one that lasted throughout his entire career, limiting his effectiveness.

At the same time, Philby often came close to having his treason discovered. James Jesus Angleton, who later became the head of the CIA,

Chief James J. Angleton

became suspicious of Philby while working with him during World War II. Several high-ranking Soviet defectors—a term that refers to people from the Soviet Union or the West who decided to switch sides and go live with their former enemies—revealed that there were high-ranking British intelligence agents who were secretly spying for the Soviet Union. For different reasons, however, Philby always managed to escape **detection**. The higher he rose in the British intelligence service, the harder it was for anyone to believe that he could be working for the Soviets. He also had many friends in the service who thought his character to be above suspicion. Still, it was always a very close call. At one point Philby's Soviet handler actually defected to the

West but, afraid for the safety of his family still in Russia, neglected to give Philby up as a traitor.

MASTER SPY

After World War II ended, it became clear that the wartime alliance between the Soviet Union and the Western powers would be a brief one. The ideological differences and distrust between the two sides were too great to overcome. Both sides worried what would happen if the other gained an advantage, so of course each worked against the other. This was the origin of the Cold War, called that because it never resulted in a direct military conflict between the Soviet Union and the United States. But though the two sides never went to war, they were both constantly involved in plots against the other. It was a conflict that defined world politics for generations, one fought largely with spies.

By the end of World War II, Philby was one of the most effective of the KGB's undercover agents. The KGB was the Soviet equivalent of the British MI6 or the American CIA. In 1947 he was assigned to be the head of British intelligence in Turkey, and he and his family moved to Istanbul. Philby was now in the very curious position of organizing operations against the Soviets and then sabotaging them! Philby at first worked to organize groups of refugees from Armenia and Georgia, both now under

KGB
materials

Soviet control. The plan was to send them back to their home countries, where they could gather intelligence. Of course, Philby betrayed them, and they were rounded up and killed soon after leaving Turkey. He was also involved in sabotaging Operation Valuable, a joint U.S.-British operation that trained soldiers to overthrow the Communist government in Albania.

In September 1949 Philby was transferred to Washington, DC. He was the chief representative of British intelligence in the United States. He was responsible for sharing intelligence between the two countries and for helping to plan joint operations. This position made Philby one of the most important members of the British intelligence community, and it put him in an extraordinary position to access American secrets.

By this point, the CIA realized that it had a leak in its system, and that it was on the British end. In fact there were several. Though Philby was the most successful of the Soviet agents working in British intelligence, there were several others. One of them was Philby's university friend Maclean, whose cover was broken when a Soviet clerk responsible for passing **encrypted** messages failed to follow the appropriate procedure. When the code was broken, it revealed information suggesting that Maclean was a Soviet agent. This information was shared with Philby, who realized he would need to arrange for Maclean's escape somehow.

Donald Duart Maclean

This problem got even worse with the arrival of Philby's old friend and fellow Soviet agent Burgess, who had been made Second Secretary at the British embassy and even lived in Philby's house. By this point, Burgess was far more of a problem for the KGB than he was a help. Years of heavy drinking had left him dangerously unstable. He quickly made himself disliked by his American counterparts because of his terrible manners, bad behavior, and general recklessness. At one point, Burgess received three speeding tickets over the course of a single day, then pleaded diplomatic immunity and asked to be let off without charge. Philby knew that if Burgess stayed around much longer, his cover would be blown.

Guy Francis de Money Burgess

Meanwhile, the net was closing in on Maclean, who had returned to London but whose guilt, in the eyes of the CIA, was all but certain. Philby sent Burgess back to Great Britain. Burgess was supposed to tell Maclean about the danger he was in, and help Maclean escape the country. Burgess returned and contacted Maclean, but the two were slow to escape. Philby discovered the exact date that Maclean was to be arrested and interrogated, and he sent a coded telegraph to Burgess that insisted that Maclean be taken out of the country immediately. On May 25, 1951, just three days before Maclean was to be arrested, he and Burgess took a boat to France, and from there went on to Moscow.

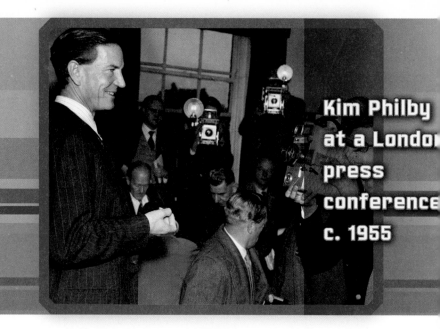

Kim Philby
at a London
press
conference
c. 1955

Burgess was only supposed to help Maclean escape, not go with him. The sudden disappearance of both of them was quite a scandal, and it left Philby in a tight spot. His close association with Burgess as well as the rumors that had swirled around him for years were enough to make him unwanted in the United States. He was shipped back to London. There he underwent a lengthy **interrogation**, but he was ultimately cleared of suspicion of being a Soviet agent. Still, his position within the British intelligence community seemed over, and he retired rather than face dismissal.

Though British intelligence had somehow failed to recognize that Philby was traitor, he still lived under a cloud of doubt. At this point, the suspicions of his treasonous activity had become public knowledge, so much so that in 1955 Philby gave a public press conference denying that he had ever been a Communist agent. Having left MI6, he was no longer of any value to the Soviets, and they cut off contact with him.

DEFECTION AND DEATH

Philby struggled to find work, trying to string together jobs as a foreign correspondent for various newspapers. In 1956, he moved to Beirut, working as a foreign correspondent. His wife, Aileen, died in 1957, but he remarried in 1958. Reports of him at this time suggest a man in deep despair, drinking heavily and on the verge of a mental breakdown.

In 1961 Anatoliy Mikhaylovich Golitsyn, a former major in the KGB, defected from a diplomatic job in Helsinki, Finland. He and his family escaped over the border to Sweden, where they were flown to the United States. In exchange for safety in the United States, Golitsyn claimed to be able to provide Soviet secrets. The most important of these was the identity of a high-ranking former MI6 agent who had long been working for the Soviets. After being debriefed by the CIA, Golitsyn was sent to London to be interrogated by MI6.

After hearing what Golitsyn had to say, MI6 gave agent Nicholas Elliott the job of traveling to Beirut and convincing Philby to provide a full confession of his activities. Philby's alcoholism had taken a disturbing turn, perhaps because he suspected that his game was almost over. During their first meeting, Elliott got Philby to admit to having worked for the Soviets, but Philby refused to sign a full confession. Before their second meeting could take place, Philby escaped. In July 1963 the Soviet Union announced that Philby was now in Moscow, and that he had been offered Soviet citizenship.

Life in Moscow proved difficult. The Soviet government did not offer him a position with the KGB, believing it was possible that he was secretly a British double agent. He was paid relatively little for the work he had done. Philby discovered the same truth that Benedict Arnold had learned two centuries earlier: No one likes a traitor. He worked on his memoir, which was published in Great Britain in 1968.

It is ultimately very difficult to determine the exact amount of damage that Philby did to the Western world as a result of his spying. The Soviets never entirely trusted him. They regarded the information that he provided as somewhat suspect, and did not always make the best use of

KGB ID card of British double agent Kim Philby

it. On the other hand, Philby was very possibly the highest-ranking double agent in the history of humankind. While working in Washington, he had been in line to become head of MI6. He unquestionably gave immense amounts of information to the Soviets: the names of foreign agents, British and U.S. spies, and details of their operations. Philby's activities directly related to the deaths of many secret agents, both British and American.

Philby's betrayal also caused significant tension between the U.S. and British intelligence communities. That so many high-ranking British spies could also be working

Memorial plaque to Kim Philby in Moscow

"Я СМОТРЮ НА ПРОЖИТУЮ ЖИЗНЬ КАК ОТДАННУЮ СЛУЖЕНИЮ ДЕЛУ, В ПРАВОТУ КОТОРОГО ИСКРЕННЕ И СТРАСТНО ВЕРЮ"

КИМ ФИЛБИ

И ГАРОЛЬД АДРИАН РАССЕЛ

1912 - 1988

for the Soviets was mind-boggling to many in the CIA. The British were increasingly seen as incompetent and untrustworthy by their U.S. counterparts, and cooperation between the two allies became strained.

Philby died in 1988, shortly before the collapse of the Soviet Union, after it had become clear that he had chosen the wrong side. By all accounts, his years in Russia were not happy ones. He was unable to find any meaningful work, drank heavily, and even attempted suicide. After his death, he was given the title Hero of the Soviet Union, the highest honor the Soviet state could award. He deserved it, having been an extraordinary help to the Soviets during the Cold War. In the West, however, he is still seen as probably the twentieth century's greatest traitor, and he deserves that recognition as well.

CONCLUSION

Each of the spies we have read about became clandestine agents for very different reasons. Some became spies because they loved their country, others because they were desperate for money. Some were thrust into spying by circumstance, while others sought it out deliberately. Some of our spies were wild, adventurous sorts, fooling the enemy with their courage and their wits. Others were quiet, cautious people, weaving plots and plans that took years to complete. By looking at them, we get a sense of what might drive a person to become a spy. We also can see the way in which the craft of spying has changed over the centuries.

For Francis Walsingham, the effective use of spies was the only way a small, relatively weak nation like England could hope to hold out against the great Spanish Empire. Because Spain was so huge and powerful, England needed to be more clever and quick. With his wide network of spies, Walsingham was able to anticipate Spain's actions and effectively plan England's responses. He found weak points in Spain's empire and exploited them, using England's superior navy to raid Spanish cities and merchant ships. Walsingham's primary motivation was duty: to his country, his queen, and his religion. He was frightened of what would happen if Catholicism became England's dominant religion, and fought it as well as he could.

Benedict Arnold is about as different a case as could be imagined. For him, spying was solely and entirely a question of personal interest. He had been a committed and even brave American patriot for most of his life, believing so strongly in the American cause that he went to war for it. As a soldier, he was not only courageous and tough but surprisingly skilled. During a time when the American army was just beginning to learn how to wage war, Arnold demonstrated a high level of skill. But his personal flaws made his virtues as a soldier unimportant. Petty, greedy, and easily offended, he sold out the country he had nearly died defending. Arnold remains a fascinating example of how a person can possess so many positive qualities yet still be brought low by his own weaknesses and lack of character.

Arnold's treason would have been particularly horrible for a woman like Belle Boyd, for whom love of homeland was everything. For Boyd, spying was the only way to strike back against the Union armies. As a woman, Boyd could not serve as a soldier, as her father and relatives did. But Boyd turned her gender to her advantage, gathering information from weak and foolish men. Whether free or imprisoned, Boyd thought of nothing but working for her beloved Confederacy. Boyd also enjoyed the thrill of being a spy, loving the excitement and adventure of the job.

Like Boyd, Virginia Hall became a spy both because of her adventurous spirit, as well as her hatred of the Nazis. She began her career as an intelligence agent years before the United States entered World War II. No doubt part of her motivation was to stop the Nazis from destroying Europe, the continent where she lived and had long loved. But part of her motivation certainly was sheer adventure. Hall loved being a spy, loved living by her wits, and loved being one step ahead of the Gestapo. She had no sooner escaped from occupied France than she was desperate to return to it. World War II represented an extraordinary opportunity for Hall to work in a profession that she otherwise would have been disqualified from, both because she was a woman and had only one leg. Unquestionably Hall's work bordered on genius. It was lucky for the Allies that they found such a skilled spy in such an unexpected form.

Hall represented the last generation of amateur spies. With the dawn of the Cold War, the need for a professional spy service became clear. Allen Dulles was primarily responsible for setting this up in the United States. His work with the OSS during World War II showed his razor-sharp mind and excellent grasp of spycraft. His time in the

CIA was more controversial. On the one hand, the CIA's interventions in Iran and Guatemala were almost certainly mistakes, ones the world is still paying for. On the other, Dulles's work to counterbalance the Soviet Union was excellent. He succeeded in setting up spy networks in the Communist countries, and in keeping them from doing the same thing in the United States.

Too bad that the British didn't do the same! Kim Philby's motivations for becoming a double agent and betraying his country are peculiar to his time. Unlike Arnold, Philby's treason was not motivated by greed or ambition. During the Cold War, political belief sometimes trumped patriotism. Philby's pro-Communist beliefs, which he came to early in life as a student, were strong enough to turn him down a decades-long path of treason. It is incredible to think that a person could live a lie for so many years and never be discovered. Certainly the extraordinary stress of the situation contributed to Philby's alcoholism and depression. To this day, it is unclear exactly how much damage Philby did to Great Britain and the United States. But there is no question that he was one of the most successful spies of the Cold War.

Of course, the end of the Cold War did not mean the end of spying! Most countries continue to have a branch of government dedicated to gathering foreign intelligence.

These days, a spy is as likely to be working on a computer as he or she is to be out in the field. More attention is paid to terrorist groups and nongovernmental organizations than in the past. But while the battlefields have changed, the basic duties of a spy have not.

GLOSSARY

Communist: a person who believes in a way of organizing the economy of a country so that all the land, property, businesses, and resources belong to the government or community, and the profits are shared by all

Conspirator: a partner in a secret plan

Covert: not openly shown

Decree: to give an order officially

Detect: to discover or notice something

Dethrone: to remove a ruler from power

Dismantle: to take apart or tear down

Encrypted: to put a message or information into a code

Fascism: a political system headed by a dictator in which the government controls business and labor and opposition is not permitted

Gallantry: an act of notable courtesy

Gestapo: the German secret police during the time when Germany was ruled by the Nazis

Guerrilla: a member of a band of persons engaged in warfare not as part of a regular army but as an independent unit

Hotbed: an environment that encourages growth or development

Idealist: a person who believes in the highest ideals, even if they seem unrealistic

Interrogation: to question someone in detail, usually in connection with a crime

Penetrate: to gain entrance to

Professionalization: an engagement in an activity for pay or as means of livelihood

Prominent: easily noticeable; distinguished

Reparations: money or materials paid or to be paid by a country losing a war to the winner to make up for damages done in the war

Saboteur: a person who performs deliberate damage or destruction especially to prevent or stop something

Secede: to withdraw from an organization as a nation or political party

Treason: the crime of being disloyal to your country by spying for another country or by helping an enemy during a war

Tribunal: a court of law

BIBLIOGRAPHY

BOOKS

Boyd, Belle. *Belle Boyd, In Camp and Prison.* London: Saunders, Otley and Co, 1865.

Budiansky, Stephen. *Her Majesty's Spymaster: Elizabeth I, Sir Francis Walsingham, and the Birth of Modern Espionage.* New York: Penguin, 2006.

Martin, James Kirby. *Benedict Arnold, Revolutionary Hero: An American Warrior Reconsidered.* New York: NYU Press, 2000.

Pearson, Judith L. *The Wolves at the Door: The True Story of America's Greatest Female Spy.* Guilford, CT: Lyons Press, 2008.

Srodes, James. *Allen Dulles: Master of Spies.* New York: Regnery, 2000.

WEBSITES

Abbott, Karen. "The Siren of the Shenandoah." *New York Times*, May 23, 2012. http://opinionator.blogs.nytimes.com/2012/05/23/the-siren-of-the-shenandoah.

Central Intelligence Agency. "Spotlight on Women's History: Virginia Hall." Last modified April 2, 2012. https://www.cia.gov/news-information/featured-story-archive/2012-featured-story-archive/virginia-hall.html.

Creighton, Linda L. "Benedict Arnold: A Traitor, but Once a Patriot." *U.S. News & World Report*, June 27, 2008. http://www.usnews.com/news/national/articles/2008/06/27/benedict-arnold-a-traitor-but-once-a-patriot.

DeMarco, Michael. "Belle Boyd (1844–1900)." *Encyclopedia Virginia*. Last modified March 31, 2011. http://www. EncyclopediaVirginia.org/Boyd_Belle_1844-1900.

Henry, William A. "Espionage No Regrets Kim Philby: 1912-1988." *Time*, May 23, 1988. http://www.time.com/time/maga-zine/article/0,9171,967442,00.html.

Tweedie, Neil. "Kim Philby: Father, husband, traitor, spy." *Telegraph* (London), January 23, 2013. http://www.telegraph. co.uk/history/9818727/Kim-Philby-Father-husband-traitor-spy. html.

ABOUT THE AUTHOR

Daniel Polansky lives in New York as an author of books for adults and a lover of history. This is his second book in the PROFILES series.

ALSO AVAILABLE

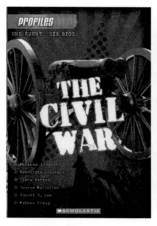

PROFILES: THE CIVIL WAR
978-0-545-23756-7

PROFILES: WORLD WAR II
978-0-545-31655-2

PROFILES: TECH TITA
978-0-545-36577-2

**PROFILES:
FREEDOM HEROINES**
978-0-545-42518-6

**PROFILES:
THE VIETNAM WAR**
978-0-545-48855-6

**PROFILES:
PEACE WARRIORS**
978-0-545-51857-4